THE WHITE ROOTS OF PEACE

*The land shall be beautiful,
the river shall have no more waves,
one may go everywhere without fear.*

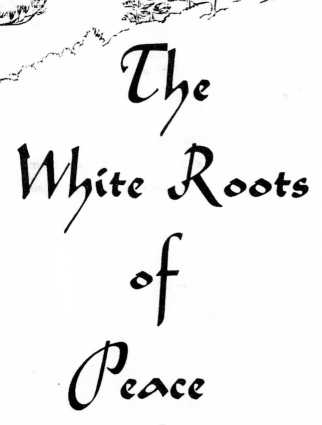

The White Roots of Peace

By

PAUL A. W. WALLACE

KENNIKAT PRESS
Port Washington, N. Y./London

132217

THE WHITE ROOTS OF PEACE

Copyright 1946 by Paul A. W. Wallace
Reissued in 1968 by Ira J. Friedman, Inc. by arrangement
with the University of Pennsylvania Press
Library of Congress Card No.: 68-18363
ISBN 0-3046-3054-X

EMPIRE STATE HISTORICAL PUBLICATIONS SERIES No. 54

To

the memory of

DEWASERAGE

(Chief William D. Loft)

who held the Mohawk name and title of

SHARENKHOWANE

in the Council of the Six Nations

Acknowledgments

THE legend of Deganawidah and the founding of the Iroquois Confederacy has for many generations been handed down among the Indians by word of mouth. Only in this generation has the full narrative of this remarkable man and his league for peace, which has endured for five hundred years, been set down in letters.

There are three main versions of the legend in English, all of which I have used in preparing the present book:

1. *The Newhouse version*, gathered and prepared by Seth Newhouse, a Canadian Mohawk, and revised by Albert Cusick, a New York Onondaga-Tuscarora. This version has been edited and published by Dr. Arthur C. Parker of the Rochester Museum in "The Constitution of the Five Nations, or the Iroquois Book of the Great Law" (*New York State Museum Bulletin*, No. 184, Albany, 1916).

2. *The Chiefs' version*, compiled by the chiefs of the Six Nations Council on the Six Nations Reserve, Ontario, 1900. This version appears in the "Traditional History of the Confederacy of the Six Nations," edited by Duncan C. Scott (*Proceedings and Transactions of the Royal Society of Canada*, Vol. 5, Ottawa, 1911).

3. *The Gibson version*, dictated in 1899 by Chief John Arthur Gibson of the Six Nations Reserve to the late J. N. B. Hewitt of the Smithsonian Institution, and revised by Chiefs Abram Charles, John Buck, Sr., and Joshua Buck, from 1900 to 1914. This version, which is still in manuscript, was translated into English in 1941 by Dr. William N. Fenton of the Bureau of American Ethnology, Smithsonian Institution, with the help of Chief Simeon Gibson.

A revision and expansion of his own earlier version was dictated by Chief John Arthur Gibson in 1912 to Alexander A. Goldenweiser of the Anthropological Division, Geological Survey, Ottawa, Canada. This is still in manuscript, untranslated, in the care of Dr. Fenton.

No single version of the legend tells a wholly consistent story. The only way to get an approximation of the original is to attempt a composite narrative, such as has been done in the following pages. Nothing in the present rendering has been invented by the writer, but where the versions differ he has used his discretion in selecting

[vii]

the incidents or the words that best convey the central motif. The startling parallel between the symbols of the old legend and the thoughts that are in the minds of all persons interested in world peace today is apparent in any perusal of the original versions.

I wish to acknowledge my great indebtedness to Dr. William N. Fenton, who has permitted me to examine his translation of the Gibson version and to incorporate excerpts from it in the text. In shaping the narrative contained in "The Legend of Deganawidah," I should have been lost without the Gibson version, which tells a more coherent story than is found in the other versions and which at the same time points the allegory with greater insight. I have in consequence leaned heavily on Dr. Fenton's translation both for incident and for dialogue, and I have relied almost wholly on his scholarly interpretation of the triple message contained in the Good News of Peace and Power. I owe further thanks to Dr. Fenton for his kindness and patience in reading my manuscript and offering many valuable criticisms and suggestions.

I am also much indebted to Dr. Arthur C. Parker for permission to quote, as I have done repeatedly in the chapters entitled "Words of Wampum," "Antlers of Authority," and "World Citizens," from the beautiful prose of "The Constitution of the Five Nations."

Acknowledgments are also due to others who have given me generous assistance in pursuit of the Deganawidah legend, especially to Dr. Frank G. Speck, Department of Anthropology, University of Pennsylvania; to Major H. C. Durston, Secretary of the Onondaga Historical Association, Syracuse, N. Y.; to Dr. Carl E. Guthe, Director, and Mr. Alvin Goodnow Whitney, Assistant Director, of the New York State Museum, Albany; and to Mr. Washington W. Loveland, Syracuse, N. Y.

Among the many secondary sources to which I have had recourse, particular mention should be made of J. N. B. Hewitt's monograph, edited by Dr. William N. Fenton, "The Requickening Address of the Iroquois Condolence Council" (*Journal of the Washington Academy of Science,* Vol. 34, No. 3, March 15, 1944), which has provided material for the chapter "Words of Wampum"; also of Horatio Hale's *The Iroquois Book of Rites* (Philadelphia, 1883) and Dr. William M. Beauchamp's "Civil, Religious and Mourning Councils and Ceremonies of Adoption of the New York Indians" (*New York State Museum Bulletin,* No. 113, Albany, 1907), both of which have provided material for the "Six Songs" (the Peace Hymn) and other parts of the Installation Ceremony in the following pages.

It was the late Chief William D. Loft of the Six Nations Reserve, a Mohawk artist and scholar of distinction, who first inspired me with the desire to probe under the surface of the Deganawidah legend, which he had told to me. In his own person Chief Loft exemplified Deganawidah's message of Peace and Power.

The Hiawatha who appears in these pages is an historical figure, and has little in common with the hero of Longfellow's *Song of Hiawatha*. Longfellow, following the ethnologist H. R. Schoolcraft (who confused the man, Hiawatha, with the god, Tarachiawagon), mistakenly attached the name of the Iroquois Hiawatha to a cycle of Ojibway Indian myths centering about the demigod Manabozho, who worked wonders on the shores of Lake Superior. Longfellow has given a sympathetic interpretation of the Indian mind. but he has added nothing to our knowledge of the Iroquois.

January 1946   P.A.W.W.

Contents

	Page
Acknowledgments	vii

THE FIVE NATIONS

Faith and Fire	3
The Tree of Peace	6

THE LEGEND OF DEGANAWIDAH

I Am Deganawidah	11
Hiawatha Sees Himself	15
The Mohawks Take Hold	18
Words of Wampum	20
Combing the Snakes Out of Atotarho's Hair	23

UNITED NATIONS

Antlers of Authority	29
World Citizens	42
The Eagle Keeps Watch	45
Twilight	54

1945

SAN FRANCISCO

We, the peoples of the United Nations, determined to save succeeding generations from the scourge of war . . .

PREAMBLE TO THE CONSTITUTION OF THE UNITED NATIONS

1450

(circa)

ONONDAGA

I am Deganawidah
and with the Five Nations' confederate lords
I plant the Tree of the Great Peace. . . .
Roots have spread out
from the Tree of the Great Peace . . . and the name of these roots is
the Great White Roots of Peace. If any man or any nation
outside of the Five Nations
shall show a desire to obey
the laws of the Great Peace . . . they may trace the roots to their
source . . . and they shall be welcomed
to take shelter beneath the Tree . . .

PREAMBLE TO THE CONSTITUTION OF THE UNITED NATIONS

THE FIVE NATIONS

Faith and Fire

THIS is the story of the founding at Onondaga (Syracuse, N. Y.), some time about the middle of the fifteenth century, of the United Nations of the Iroquois, the famous Indian confederacy that provided a model for, and an incentive to, the transformation of the thirteen colonies into the United States of America.

"It would be a strange thing," wrote Benjamin Franklin, "if Six Nations of ignorant savages should be capable of forming a scheme for such a union, and be able to execute it in such a manner as that it has subsisted ages and appears indissoluble; and yet that a like union should be impracticable for ten or a dozen English colonies to whom it is more necessary and must be more advantageous, and who cannot be supposed to want an equal understanding of their interests."

In Franklin's day the Six Nations, as the Iroquois then called themselves, were the greatest Indian power on the American continent. The original Five Nations—Mohawks, Oneidas, Onondagas, Cayugas, and Senecas, with whom a sixth, the Tuscaroras, had been joined since about 1710—dominated all surrounding tribes, and, from their homeland in northern New York, between the Hudson and Niagara Rivers, maintained a *pax iroquoia* that in their most heroic days had extended from what is now New England to the Illinois region and from the Ottawa River to Chesapeake Bay.

It was not by force alone that the Iroquois held this vast region under their Peace. It was by statesmanship, by a profound understanding of the principles of peace itself. They knew that any real peace must be based on justice and a healthy reasonableness. They knew also that peace will endure only if men recognize the sovereignty of a common law and are prepared to back that law with force—not chiefly for the purpose of punishing those who have disturbed the peace, but rather for the purpose of preventing such disturbance by letting all men know, *in advance* of any contingency, that the law will certainly prevail.

Behind their statesmanship lay a will to peace among the people, without which all the wisdom of their chiefs gathered in the Great

Council at Onondaga would have been futile. It was in the handling of this problem, how to maintain a popular will to peace, that the Iroquois made their greatest contribution to government—a contribution that it may be profitable for us to examine today, since there is now no greater problem confronting global statesmanship than that of maintaining this popular will to peace despite increasing tensions in an ever-more-narrowly-jostling world society.

Among the Five Nations it is evident that the peace incentive was a complex thing, rooted in many motives, chief among which were three: the example of two culture heroes, a unique interpretation of the meaning of peace itself, and a set of peace symbols that seized the imagination and so gave both interpretation and example a power to drive the human will.

The two culture heroes, whose deeds and words have been treasured through the centuries in a traditional narrative of great beauty, were two men of peace, Deganawídah and his spokesman, Hiawatha.

Deganawidah, a Huron Indian by birth but a Mohawk by adoption, was the man of faith, the man of purpose, who gave a New Mind and a new way of life to his people. His name, it is believed by some, means the Master of Things, for he implemented his visions with a machinery of government that gave them substance.

Hiawatha, an Onondaga Indian by birth but like Deganawidah a Mohawk by adoption, was the man of fire, the man of feeling, whose eloquence won converts to Deganawidah's visions. His name means He Who Combs, for he combed the twists out of men's perverted minds.

Dewaseráge (Chief William D. Loft), the Mohawk scholar to whom so much in this book is owing, has expressed the opinion that the name Deganawidah means "Double Row of Teeth," and that this appellation explains the physical impediment that caused Deganawidah to appoint Hiawatha to speak for him.

Hiawatha, the poet, is popularly believed to have invented wampum, that substitute for writing made of small shell beads threaded in symbolic designs on strings or belts, and with it to have instituted the beautiful mourning and other council ritual of the Iroquois. Deganawidah, the man of legal mind, gave his people a constitution. Together they were, as Dr. Arthur C. Parker, descendant of an ancient Seneca family, calls them, "the Blackstones of their people," who invested the customs of five distinct nations with the power of law, and brought these nations into a union cemented by such powerful sanctions of law, custom, and religion as served to make it all but indestructible.

"Through the law as a guiding force," writes Dr. Parker, "and through the heroes as ideals, the Iroquois have persisted as a people."

The task of disentangling fact from folklore in the story of these heroes is not attempted here. No effort is made to distinguish between what the Iroquois actually received from Deganawidah and Hiawatha while they lived and what the popular imagination after their death gave back by way of tribute to their memory. For of course these culture heroes, as we see them now in the legend, are in part the product of imaginative processes which their living originals had set in motion.

The purpose in these pages is to show the legend in its dynamic unity: to let it appear as the constructive force it actually was, one that seized on the minds of the Iroquois, directed their moral energies to the preservation of the Peace, and so gave them an influence on history out of all proportion to their numbers.

The story of Deganawidah and Hiawatha virtually constituted the Iroquois Bible. In it, if anywhere, are to be found the moral incentives that enabled them to make their Great Peace lasting.

The Tree of Peace

THE Indians of the Five Nations were a practical people. They lived in good houses, built walled towns for their protection, and supported themselves by the cultivation of the soil. Corn, beans, and squash, the "Three Sisters," formed the staple of their diet, with venison and fish in season. Their clothing was adequate and modest. They gave themselves steam baths in specially constructed huts by pouring water on heated stones. In war their discipline and skilled leadership made up for lack of numbers. In private life they got on well with one another, their games, dances, and conversation being seldom interrupted by personal quarrels. In public life they excelled in political organization and the forensic arts that went with it.

They were not, for the most part, of a philosophical turn of mind, their abilities being rather of an Hebraic than of an Hellenic cast. They were better in practice than in theory. Their religion was sounder than their theology, their political institutions maturer than their political science. The only science in which they excelled was that of human relationships.

Nowhere is this practical bent of mind better seen than in the way they talked about peace. Peace was not, as they conceived it, a negative thing, the mere absence of war or an interval between wars, to be recognized only as the stepchild of the law—as unfortunately has been the case with most western peoples, among whom the laws of peace, in the international field, have been recognized by jurists as an afterthought to the laws of war.

To the Iroquois, peace *was* the law. They used the same word for both. Peace (the Law) was righteousness in action, the practice of justice between individuals and nations. If they ever recognized it as a mystic presence, like the light which Shelley conceived as giving "grace and truth to life's unquiet dream," they found it, not in some imagined retreat from the world, but in human institutions, especially in a good government. Their own Confederacy, which they named the Great Peace, was sacred. The chiefs who administered the League were their priests.

[6]

In their thought peace was so inseparable from the life of man that they had no separate term by which to denominate it. It was thought of and spoken of in terms of its component elements: as Health and Reason (soundness of body and sanity of mind), Law (justice codified to meet particular cases), and Authority (which gives confidence that justice will prevail).

Peace was a way of life, characterized by wisdom and graciousness.

The root word which, in various combinations, is used to express "peace" in the Iroquois tongue, is the same as that used for "noble" and "the Lord" in their translations of the Bible. Peace was to their mind nobility, the Great Good. Even such renderings of the term in English are too abstract to catch their way of looking at it. Peace was the Good expressed in action, that is, the good life. It was also, in their thought, the Ideal Commonwealth—not *Utopia* (No Place), but *Kayánerénhkowa* (the Great Peace) established so firmly at Onondaga.

Their symbol for this Peace was a tree, and the tree had roots in the earth.

The power of symbols is profound, especially among an active and emotional people; for symbols are a means by which practical persons, shy of metaphysics and impatient of theory, are enabled to apprehend great ideas, take them to heart, and put them to work. The Iroquois fed their minds and guided their actions by means of symbols. When Deganawidah stood before the first council of the United Nations at Onondaga and planted the Tree of the Great Peace, he planted in the hearts of his people a symbol that was to give power and permanence to their union.

Like the spires on our churches, the Great White Pine which "pierces the sky" and "reaches the sun," lifted the thoughts of the Iroquois to the meanings of peace—the Good News which they believed the Great Spirit, the Iroquois god Tarachiawágon (Holder of the Heavens), had sent Deganawidah to impart to them.

In general the Tree signified the Law, that is, the constitution, which expressed the terms of their union. But there were other important elements in the symbol.

The Branches signified shelter, the protection and security that people found in union under the shadow of the Law.

The Roots, which stretched to the four quarters of the earth, signified the extension of the Law, the Peace, to embrace all mankind. Other nations, not yet members of the League, would see these roots as they grew outward, and, if they were people of goodwill, would desire to follow them to their source and take shelter with others under the Tree.

The Eagle That Sees Afar, which Deganawidah placed on the very summit of the Tree, signified watchfulness. "And the meaning of placing an Eagle on the top of the Tree," said Deganawidah, "is to watch the roots which extend to the North and to the South and to the East and to the West, and the Eagle will discover if any evil is approaching your Confederacy, and will scream and give the alarm and all the Nations of the Confederacy at once shall hear the alarm and come to the front."

The Eagle, said Deganawidah, "shall have your power." It was a reminder to his people that the best political contrivance that the wit of man can devise is impotent to keep the peace unless a watchful people stands always on guard to defend it.

Then Deganawidah uprooted the Tree and under it disclosed a Cavern through which ran a stream of water, passing out of sight into unknown regions under the earth. Into this current he cast the weapons of war, the hatchets and war-clubs, saying, "We here rid the earth of these things of an Evil Mind." Then, replacing the Tree, "Thus," he said, "shall the Great Peace be established, and hostilities shall no longer be known between the Five Nations, but peace to the United People."

It was a simple but effective symbol he had given them in the Tree of Peace, clear in outline, suggestive, and easily remembered. It was inspiring and yet at the same time it was familiar and friendly to people who knew the forest as their home. To the man of the Five Nations, the pine in the valley through which his trail passed spoke the message of Deganawidah: Hold fast to friends, for in union there is strength; welcome the stranger and give him shelter, for he may become a prop to your house; bury your hates and let them be forgotten, for if old stories are to be revived there can never be an end to war.

And the eagle which the man of the Five Nations saw circling in the sky above him was a reminder that the price of peace, as of liberty, is eternal vigilance.

THE LEGEND OF DEGANAWIDAH

I Am Deganawidah

DEGANAWIDAH is said to have been born at a Huron settlement, Tkahaánaye, on the north shore of Lake Ontario not far from the site of the modern Kingston, Ontario.

Before his birth the name of the child was disclosed to his grandmother, as was the way among the Iroquois, in a dream.

A messenger from the Great Spirit stood before the grandmother and said:

"It is the will of the Master of Life, the Holder of the Heavens, that thy daughter, a virgin, shall bear a child. He shall be called Deganawidah, the Master of Things, for he brings with him the Good News of Peace and Power. Care for him well, thou and thy daughter, for he has a great office to perform in the world."

"What is the child's office to be?" asked the grandmother.

"His office is to bring peace and life to the people on earth," replied the messenger. "After he is grown to manhood, see that thou place no obstacle in his way when he desires to leave home to spread the New Mind among the nations."

So when Deganawidah was become a man, he said one day to his mother and grandmother:

"I shall now build my canoe, for the time has come for me to set out on my mission in the world. Know that far away, on lakes and many rivers, I go seeking the council smoke of nations beyond this lake, holding my course toward the sunrise. It is my business to stop the shedding of blood among human beings."

When he had built his canoe and, with the help of his mother and grandmother, had brought it to the water, he bade them farewell.

"Do not look for me to return," he said, "for I shall not come again this way. Should you wish to know if all is well with me, go to the hilltop yonder where stands a single tree. Cut at the tree with your hatchets, and, if blood flows from the wound, you will know that I have perished and my work has failed. But if no blood flows, all is well, my mission is successful."

"But the canoe is made of stone," said his grandmother. "It will not float."

"It will float," replied Deganawidah. "This shall be a sign that my words are true."

He entered the canoe, and it moved swiftly out into the Lake.

Deganawidah crossed Lake Ontario (Sganyadaií-yo, the Beautiful Great Lake) and approached the land of the Iroquois. As the shore line took form to his eyes, he scanned it for signs of ascending smoke, but saw none; for indeed the settlements at that time were all back among the hills, whose steep sides offered protection to stockaded villages against their enemies. Those were evil days, for the five Iroquois peoples were all at war with one another, and made themselves an easy prey to their fierce Algonquin enemies, the Adirondacks, who came down on them from what is now northern New England, and the Wolves or Mahicans of Hudson's River who assailed them on the east.

As Deganawidah neared the land, he saw the figures of men, small in the distance, running along the shore; for some hunters had seen a sparkle of light from the white stone canoe and ran to see what it could be. Whereupon Deganawidah turned his canoe toward them, and, making land swiftly, beached the canoe and climbed the bank and stood before them.

Looking about him, he saw that the region was bare of cornfields.

"Is there no settlement here?" he asked.

"No," they replied.

"Then what has brought you to this desolate place?"

"We are hunters," they said. "We have come away from our hill settlement because there is strife in it."

"Go back to your settlement," said Deganawidah. "Tell your chief that the Good News of Peace and Power has come, and that there will be no more strife in his village. If he asks whence peace is to come, say to him, 'It will come.'"

"Who art thou that speakest thus to us?"

"I am Deganawidah," he replied. "I come from the west and I go toward the sunrise. I am called Deganawidah in the world."

When he turned and went down the bank to enter his canoe, the men wondered as they looked, for they saw that the canoe was made of white stone.

The hunters, returning to the settlement as Deganawidah had bidden them, went to their chief and said to him, "The Good News of Peace and Power has come."

"What is this you are saying?" said the chief.

"There will be no more strife in the settlement."

"Who told you this?"

They replied, "He is called Deganawidah in the world."

"Where did you see him?"

"On the Beautiful Great Lake. He came from the west and he goes toward the sunrise. His canoe is made of white stone and it moves swiftly."

Then the chief began to wonder at the news. His town was at war, and his people within the stockades were hungry and quarreling among themselves.

"Whence can peace come?" he said.

They replied, "It will come."

Then said the chief: "Truly this is a wonderful thing. Such news of itself will bring peace to the settlement if once men believe it. All will be glad and at ease in their minds to know that this thing will be."

So Deganawidah passed from settlement to settlement, finding that men desired peace and would practise it if they knew for a certainty that others would practise it, too.

But first, after leaving the hunters, Deganawidah sought the house of a certain woman who lived by the warriors' path which passed between the east and the west.

When Deganawidah arrived, the woman placed food before him and, after he had eaten, asked him his message.

"I carry the Mind of the Master of Life," he replied, "and my message will bring an end to the wars between east and west."

"How will this be?" asked the woman, who wondered at his words, for it was her custom to feed the warriors passing before her door on their way between the east and the west.

"The Word that I bring," he said, "is that all peoples shall love one another and live together in peace. This message has three parts: Righteousness and Health and Power—Gáiwoh, Skénon, Gashasdénshaa. And each part has two branches.

"Righteousness means justice practised between men and between nations; it means also a desire to see justice prevail.

"Health means soundness of mind and body; it also means peace, for that is what comes when minds are sane and bodies cared for.

"Power means authority, the authority of law and custom, backed by such force as is necessary to make justice prevail; it means also religion, for justice enforced is the will of the Holder of the Heavens and has his sanction."

"Thy message is good," said the woman; "but a word is nothing until it is given form and set to work in the world. What form shall this message take when it comes to dwell among men?"

"It will take the form of the longhouse," replied Deganawidah, "in which there are many fires, one for each family, yet all live as one household under one chief mother. Hereabouts are five nations, each with its own council fire, yet they shall live together as one household in peace. They shall be the Kanonsiónni, the Longhouse. They shall have one mind and live under one law. Thinking shall replace killing, and there shall be one commonwealth."

"That is indeed a good message," said the woman. "I take hold of it. I embrace it."

"Now it shall come to pass in that Longhouse," said Deganawidah, "that the women shall possess the titles of chiefship. They shall name the chiefs. That is because thou, my Mother, wert the first to accept the Good News of Peace and Power. Henceforth thou shalt be called Jigónhsasee, New Face, for thy countenance evinces the New Mind, and thou shalt be known as the Mother of Nations."

Then Jigonhsasee said: "I am a woman and do not make war. But the work I do is to feed the warriors passing my door on their way between east and west. They, too, must accept the New Mind or there will be no end to killing. Where wilt thou first take thy message?"

"I go toward the sunrise," replied Deganawidah.

"The direction thou takest is dangerous," said Jigonhsasee. "That way stands the house of a man who eats humans."

"That is the business I go about," said Deganawidah, "to bring such evils to an end, so that all men may go about from place to place without fear."

Hiawatha Sees Himself

WHEN Deganawidah came to the house of the "man who eats humans," he climbed to the roof and lay flat on his chest beside the smoke hole. There he waited until the man came home carrying a human body, which he put in his kettle on the fire. Deganawidah moved closer and looked straight down.

At that moment the man bent over the kettle. Seeing a face looking up at him, he was amazed. It was Deganawidah's face he saw reflected in the water, but the man thought it was his own. There was in it such wisdom and strength as he had never seen before nor ever dreamed that he possessed.

The man moved back into a corner of the house, and sat down and began to think.

"This is a most wonderful thing," he said. "Such a thing has never happened before as long as I have lived in this house. I did not know I was like that. It was a great man who looked at me out of the kettle. I shall look again and make sure that what I have seen is true."

He went over to the kettle, and there again was the face of a great man looking up at him.

"It is true," he said. "It is my own face in which I see wisdom and righteousness and strength. But it is not the face of a man who eats humans. I see that it is not like me to do that."

He took the kettle out of the house, and emptied it by the roots of an upturned tree.

"Now I have changed my habits," he said. "I no longer kill humans and eat their flesh. But that is not enough. The mind is more difficult to change. I cannot forget the suffering I have caused, and I am become miserable."

Then the man felt his loneliness and said, "Perhaps someone will come here, some stranger it may be, who will tell me what I must do to make amends for all the human beings I have made to suffer."

When he returned to the house, he met Deganawidah, who had climbed down from the roof, and they entered and sat down across the fire from each other.

[15]

"Today I have seen a strange thing," said the man. "I saw a face looking at me out of the kettle in this house where I live. It was my own face. but it was not the face of the man who has lived here. It was the face of a great man, but I am become miserable."

"Truly," said Deganawidah, "what has happened this day makes a wonderful story. Thou hast changed the very pattern of thy life. The New Mind has come to thee, namely Righteousness and Health and Power. And thou art miserable because the New Mind does not live at ease with old memories. Heal thy memories by working to make justice prevail. Bring peace to those places where thou hast done injury to man. Thou shalt work with me in advancing the Good News of Peace and Power."

"That is a good message," said the man. "I take hold, I grasp it. Now what work is there for us both to do?"

"First, let us eat together," said Deganawidah. "I will go into the woods for our food. Do thou go to the stream and fetch water for the kettle. But be careful. Dip with the current. One must never go against the forces of nature."

When Deganawidah came back from the woods, he bore on his shoulders a deer with large antlers.

"It is on the flesh of the deer," said Deganawidah, "that the Holder of the Heavens meant men to feed themselves, and the deer's antlers shall be placed on their heads. Great men shall wear the antlers of authority, and by these emblems all men shall know those who administer the new order of Peace and Power which I am come to establish."

"What will this new order be called?" asked the man.

"When it is completed," replied Deganawidah, "it will be called by these names: Kanonsionni, the Longhouse, the League; and Kayanerenhkowa, the Great Peace, or the Great Law. Men shall live together in one community, as in the longhouse, and they shall live in peace because they live under one law."

Now not far from that place there lived a chief of the Onondagas named Atotárho who was a great wizard and evil. He was so cruel that he killed and devoured all men who approached him uninvited, and so strong that the birds flying over his lodge fell dead at his feet if he waved his arms. He had a twisted body and a twisted mind, and his hair was a mass of tangled snakes. No man liked to see him, and the sound of his voice carried terror through the land; but his power was mighty, and Deganawidah knew that the cause of peace could not be completed without him.

"Thou shalt visit this man Atotarho," said Deganawidah, "for he is of thy people, the Onondagas. He is ugly, but we need him. When he asks thee for thy message, say, 'It is Righteousness and Health, and when men take hold of it they will stop killing one another and live in peace.'

"He will not listen to thee, but drive thee away. Yet thou shalt come to him again and at last prevail. Thou shalt be called Hiawatha, He Who Combs, for thou shalt comb the snakes out of Atotarho's hair."

The Mohawks Take Hold

BEFORE he continued his journey toward the sunrise, seeking the smoke of peoples, Deganawidah visited Atotarho to prepare his mind for Hiawatha's message. He found the wizard seated on a great rock in a glen.

"I am come to prepare thy mind," said Deganawidah, "for the Good News of Peace and Power. When men accept it, they will stop killing, and bloodshed will cease from the land."

Atotarho's head was covered with snakes and his body was crooked. He loved disorder and hated peace, but he did not say so, for his mind was twisted and his workings were evil and indirect.

"When will this be?" he cried: "Hwe-do-né-e-e-e-eh?"

He drew out the last sound in a howl that carried far through the forest, striking fear into all who heard it. It was the mocking cry of the doubter who killed men by destroying their faith.

"It will be," replied Deganawidah. "I shall come again, with Hiawatha, who will comb the snakes out of thy hair."

Thence Deganawidah took his course toward the sunrise, toward the land of the Kanienga, the Flint Nation, or Mohawks. By the Lower Falls of the Mohawk River (Cohoes, N. Y.), Deganawidah made camp, and in the evening sat beneath a tall tree and smoked his pipe.

A man of the Kanienga passing by saw him and asked, "Who art thou?"

"I am Deganawidah," he replied. "The Great Creator from whom we are all descended sent me to establish the Great Peace among you."

"There is no peace here," said the man. "But I will take thee to my village, and thou shalt explain this message to the people."

So Deganawidah presented the Good News of Peace and Power, of Reason and Law, to the Mohawks in that place, and the people were glad, for they found it a good message.

But their chiefs were cautious and held back.

The Chief Warrior said to Deganawidah: "Thou speakest well. Reason and law and peace are good things. But east and west of our village are powerful tribes who are always at war with us. Whence can peace come?"

"It will come," said Deganawidah, "with the Words of the Law. The Great Binding Law—that is Peace."

Then said the Chief Warrior to the people: "What this man says is good, but is it true? Let him give us a sign. Let him climb to the top of a tall tree by the falls, and we shall cut it down over the cliff. If he live to see the sunrise, we shall accept his message."

So all moved to the place where the tree stood beside the falls.

"If thou livest to see tomorrow's sunrise," said the Chief Warrior, "we shall take hold of thy message."

Deganawidah climbed the tree to the topmost branch. Then the Mohawks cut the tree down so that it fell over the cliff into the water. The people watched to see if Deganawidah came up, but there was no sign of him.

"Let us return at sunrise," said the Chief Warrior, and the people went back to their village for the night.

Next morning, before sunrise, a man of the Kanienga coming to the place by the falls where the tree had fallen, saw at a little distance across the cornfields a column of smoke rising, and going toward it he saw a man seated by his fire. It was Deganawidah.

When the man returned to the village and told what he had seen, the people came out and brought Deganawidah back to the place of council.

The Chief Warrior spoke. "Yesterday," he said, "I was in great doubt, for words, however good, do not always betoken the thing that is. Now I am in doubt no longer. This is a great man, who reveals to us the Mind of the Master of Life. Let us accept his message. Let us take hold of the Good News of Peace and Power."

Then said Deganawidah: "The day is early and young, and so also is the New Mind young and tender. And as the new sun rises and proceeds surely on its course in the sky, so also shall the Young Mind prevail and prosper among men. There shall be peace. Your children and your grandchildren and those whose faces are yet beneath the ground shall live under the sky without fear."

Thus the Mohawks were the first nation to take hold of the Great Peace. They were the founders of the League.

Words of Wampum

MEANWHILE Hiawatha had met failure among the Onondagas. The people were with him; they accepted the New Mind and desired to take hold of the Peace. But Hiawatha could make no headway against their chief, Atotarho.

Three times Hiawatha called a council. Three times the councilors set out to visit Atotarho and straighten his twisted mind. But three times the wizard's evil power rushed out to meet them. Three times their councils were dissolved. Some of the Onondagas, approaching Atotarho in their canoes, were drowned by the waves. Others were set fighting among themselves. Blood was shed. Hiawatha was not injured in his body, but he was wounded in his mind by the obstructions placed in his path.

One day he heard Atotarho's voice crying out of the air, "Hiawatha-a-a-a-a-a!" and he was troubled, for he knew that mischief was hatching.

Soon Hiawatha's three daughters were taken ill, one after the other, and all died. Hiawatha's grief bowed him down.

"I shall be unable to perform the work of the Good Mind," he said, "because of this awful thing that has befallen me."

Seeing him thus depressed, the people came to comfort him, and they arranged a game of lacrosse to lift his mind. But when a mysterious bird dropped out of the sky, and the crowd, pursuing it, trampled his wife to death, his grief overcame him. He "split the sky" (struck south) and left the land of the Onondagas.

So began the journey that figures so prominently in Iroquois legend. Not far up among the mountains from Onondaga (Syracuse) Hiawatha came to the Tully Lakes, crossing one of them, it is said, with dry moccasins because the ducks at his request had lifted the water for him to pass.

Picking up shells from the lake bottom, he threaded them on three strings of jointed rushes as a mark of his grief. At night when he built his fire at that place, which he named Ohondogónwa, the Land of Rushes, he held the three strings in his hand and said:

"This would I do if I found anyone burdened with grief even as

I am. I would take these shell strings in my hand and console them. The strings would become words and lift away the darkness with which they are covered. Holding these in my hand, my words would be true."

Every night when he made his fire, he set up two crotched sticks, placed another across them, and from it he hung the three strings of shells. Then he sat down and repeated his saying:

"This would I do if I found anyone burdened with grief even as I am. I would take these shell strings in my hand and console them. The strings would become words and lift away the darkness with which they are covered. Holding these in my hand, my words would be true."

For many days Hiawatha was a wanderer, moving through the forest without direction, sometimes south and sometimes north and sometimes east.

"I can only rove about," he said, "since now I have cast myself away from my people."

When he came to settlements, the smoke from his fire at evening was seen at the wood's edge, but no one came to console him. Men knew that it was Hiawatha, for they had heard of his departure from Onondaga. They knew, too, that he was destined to go to the country of the Flint Nation; for a runner had come from the south, from a nation by the seashore, telling of a seer in that country who had dreamed that a man from the north should meet a man from the west in the country of the Kanienga, the Mohawks, and that together they should establish a Great Peace.

But no one took up the strings of wampum to condole with him.

He built himself a canoe and paddled down the Mohawk River till, on the twenty-third day after his departure from the Onondagas, he came to the village by the Lower Falls, and built his fire at the wood's edge.

That night Deganawidah went to the place where the smoke from Hiawatha's fire was seen rising.

As he approached, he heard the voice of Hiawatha, saying:

"This would I do if I found anyone burdened with grief even as I am. I would take these shell strings in my hand and condole with them. The strings would become words and lift away the darkness with which they are covered. Holding these in my hand, my words would be true."

Then Deganawidah came forward and, taking the strings from

the horizontal pole and holding them, with others he had made, in his hand, he spoke, string by string, the several Words of the Requickening Address, used for all generations since in the Iroquois Condolence Ceremony.

"I wipe away the tears from thy face," said Deganawidah, "using the white fawn-skin of pity. . . . I make it daylight for thee. . . . I beautify the sky. Now shalt thou do thy thinking in peace when thine eyes rest on the sky, which the Perfector of our Faculties, the Master of All Things, intended should be a source of happiness to man."

Thus was Hiawatha's mind cleared of its grief.

"Now," said Deganawidah, "Reason has returned; thy judgment is firm again. Thou art ready to advance the New Mind. Let us together make the laws of the Great Peace, which shall abolish war."

So when the Great Law was completed, and for each item a string or belt of wampum had been provided to enable them to remember it the more easily, Hiawatha and Deganawidah carried the Words of the Great Peace to the nations of the west: the Oneidas, Onondagas, Cayugas, and Senecas.

As they went, they sang the Peace Hymn, the *Hai! Hai!*:

> Hail! Hail! Hail!
> To the Great Peace bring we greeting . . .

That song is still sung, modified by the nostalgia of later genera-tions for the golden age of the League's birth, whenever the ancient ritual is invoked for the installation of chiefs in the Great Peace.

Combing the Snakes Out of Atotarho's Hair

A CCOMPANIED by chiefs of the Mohawk nation, Deganawidah and Hiawatha first approached the Oneidas, the People of the Standing Stone, whom they had little difficulty in persuading to accept the Great Peace sponsored by their powerful neighbors, the Mohawks.

Beyond the Oneidas lay the Onondagas, but the paralyzing cry of Atotarho, "Hwe-do-ne-e-e-e-eh? When will this be?" forced them to leave the Onondagas, the People of the Hills, and pass on to the Great Pipe People, the Cayugas.

The mild-mannered Cayugas, always quick to help their fellow humans, and a little fearful at their own situation between such powerful peoples as the Onondagas and Senecas, were glad enough to take hold of the Great Peace. So now, with three nations at their back, Deganawidah and Hiawatha returned to the politically minded Onondagas, and were able to convince their chiefs (all but Atotarho) that it would be well to join. Then, accompanied by the chiefs of four nations, Mohawks, Oneidas, Onondagas, and Cayugas, they carried the Peace Hymn to Canandaigua Lake, where they persuaded the two branches of the People of the Great Hill, the Senecas, warlike and independent though they were, to compose their rivalries and enter the Longhouse.

"Now," said Deganawidah, "we must seek the fire and look for the smoke of Atotarho. He alone stands across our path. His mind is twisted and there are seven crooks in his body. These must be straightened if the League is to endure."

So Deganawidah returned to Onondaga Lake and assembled the chiefs of five nations in the woods beside it.

"Come," said Deganawidah to Hiawatha, "thou and I alone shall go first to the Great Wizard. I shall sing the Peace Song and thou shalt explain the Words of the Law, holding the wampum in thy hand. If then we straighten his mind, the Longhouse will be completed and our work accomplished."

Accordingly the two put their canoe into the lake and dipped their paddles.

As they neared the middle of the lake, they heard the voice of Atotarho, "Asonke-né-e-e-e-eh? Is it not yet?"

"Truly," said Hiawatha, "the man is impatient."

The wind blew and the waves struck angrily against the canoe as again they heard Atotarho's cry rush out to meet them: "Asonke-ne-e-e-e-eh! It is not yet!" But Deganawidah put his strength into his paddle, and in a few moments they beached their canoe at what is now known as Hiawatha Point, on the east shore of the lake, climbed the bank, and stood before the wizard.

"Behold!" said Hiawatha. "We two are come."

"Who are you?" demanded Atotarho.

"Hast thou not heard," responded Hiawatha, "of two who were to come to thee?"

"I have heard," answered Atotarho, "that Hiawatha and Deganawidah were on their way."

"Yea, truly," said Hiawatha, "and now we two are here."

"I have waited a long time impatiently."

"Thy impatience has caused our delay," said Hiawatha.

Then, holding the strings of lake wampum in his hand, he continued:

"These are the Words of the Great Law. On these Words we shall build the House of Peace, the Longhouse with five fires that is yet one household. These are the Words of Righteousness and Health and Power."

"What is this foolishness about houses and righteousness and health?" said Atotarho.

Then Deganawidah spoke his message:

"The Words we bring constitute the New Mind, which is the will of Tarachiawagon, the Holder of the Heavens. There shall be Righteousness when men desire justice, Health when men obey reason, Power when men accept the Great Law. These things shall be given form in the Longhouse, Kanonsionni, where five nations shall live in quiet as one family. At this very place, Atotarho, where the chiefs of five nations will assemble, I shall plant the Great Tree of Peace, and its roots shall extend to far places of the earth so that all mankind may have the shelter of the Great Law."

Atotarho said, "What is that to me?"

"Thou thyself," said Deganawidah, "shalt tend the council fire of the Five Nations, the Fire That Never Dies. And the smoke of that fire shall reach the sky and be seen of all men."

"Who shall bring this about?" asked Atotarho.

"Thou shalt, if thou desirest it. Thou shalt be the Head Chief of the Five Nations."

"Of course I desire this thing," said Atotarho, "if there be anything in it. But thou art a dreamer. Where is power to bring it to pass? Asonke-ne-e-e-e-e-eh! It is not yet!"

At that Hiawatha and Deganawidah returned as they had come across the lake to where the chiefs were waiting for them on the far shore.

"Make haste," said Deganawidah. "This is the time!"

They all put their canoes into the lake and paddled across. As they neared the middle, they heard the voice of Atotarho rush out to meet them, crying, "Asonke-ne-e-e-e-e-eh! It is not yet!" The wind lifted the waves against the canoes, but they put their strength into their paddles and, before the voice had died away, they stood before Atotarho.

"Behold!" said Deganawidah. "Here is Power. These are the Five Nations. Their strength is greater than thy strength. But their voice shall be thy voice when thou speakest in council, and all men shall hear thee. This shall be thy strength in future: the will of a united people."

Then the mind of Atotarho was made straight, and Hiawatha combed the snakes out of his hair.

Deganawidah laid his hand on Atotarho's body and said: "The work is finished. Thy mind is made straight; thy head is now combed; the seven crooks have been taken from thy body. Now thou, too, hast a New Mind. Thou shalt henceforth preside over the Council, and thou shalt strive in all ways to make reason and the peaceful mind prevail. Thy voice shall be the voice of the Great Law. All men shall hear thee and find peace."

Then Deganawidah placed antlers on the heads of the chiefs in sign of their authority, and gave them the Words of the Law.

UNITED NATIONS

Antlers of Authority

A S WE pass from legend to history with the story of that first
Council by Onondaga Lake, at which Deganawidah presented
the Five Nations with a constitution (which still lives), we natu-
rally ask the question, "When did this happen?"

The answer is not as simple and clear as we could wish it to be.
The bringing together of the five separate parts of the League took,
according to the legend, five days (i.e., five years). Actually the
Completed Longhouse had taken much longer in the building,
decades or even generations. To set a precise date for the final
consolidation of the Confederacy seems impossible. The Iroquois
themselves say it happened "a long time ago"—*In the dark backward
and abysm of time.*

Chief William D. Loft once told me that when the first white
man to question the Iroquois about the League asked, "When was
this founded?" the Indians replied: "We can only tell you this way.
The Kanonsionni was already born and working when you people
first came to this country."

Some recent historians have set the approximate date at 1570.
There is some evidence for that date, but it is by no means con-
clusive, and the spirit of the legends and ceremonies of the Iroquois
must be set against it. The founding of the League is the central
theme in Iroquois story and song and ritual, and that event is
referred to today among the Indians as something of great antiquity.
It was so spoken of during the nineteenth century in the work of the
anthropologists Morgan and Hale, during the eighteenth century
in the letters of Conrad Weiser, Pennsylvania's ambassador to
Onondaga, and during the seventeenth century in the reports of the
Jesuit missionaries. The League was called ancient in the earliest
written records.

When Conrad Weiser in 1743 attended a meeting of the Onondaga
Council, at which the founding of the League was rehearsed in
song, he referred to the founders as "Ancient Chiefs." In 1691
Father Milet, a Jesuit missionary captured and adopted by the Five
Nations, was given, as we read in the *Jesuit Relations*, the "ancient
name" of one of "the first founders of the Iroquois republic,"

Otasseté, one who had been regarded "from all antiquity" *(de toute anciennenté)* as a mainstay of the nation. "From all antiquity" is had been called the Longhouse or Completed Cabin "from the surely too strong a term for a period of only 121 years (1570 to 1691). In 1654 another of the Jesuit Fathers noted that the League earliest times" *(de tout temps)*—again too strong a term for a period in this case of only eighty-four years.

Horatio Hale, writing in 1881, expressed the opinion that the League had been founded about the middle of the fifteenth century. When in 1900 a committee of chiefs on the Six Nations Reserve wrote down the story of the founding of the League as it had been handed down to them, they set the date as far back as 1390.

In view of the air of antiquity which already hung over the League when it first came under the recorded observation of white men, it seems that an earlier date than 1570, possibly Hale's 1450 or thereabouts, may be taken as the approximate date of the founding.

o　　o　　o　　o　　o

The grass is still green on the meadow overlooking Hiawatha Point where Deganawidah placed antlers on the heads of the chiefs of the Five United Nations.

After investing them thus with the symbols of their authority, he gave them the Words of the Great Law. The speech which tradition ascribes to him on that occasion, preserved through the memory of successive generations of official Wampum Keepers, still stands as the constitution of the Five Nations.

"I am Deganawidah," it begins, in the Newhouse version edited by Dr. Arthur C. Parker of the Rochester Museum, "and with the Five Nations' Confederate Lords I plant the Tree of the Great Peace. I plant it in your territory, Atotarho, and the Onondaga Nation, in the territory of you who are Firekeepers.

"I name the tree the Tree of the Great Long Leaves [i.e., the Great White Pine, according to Dr. William N. Fenton of the Smithsonian Institution]. Under the shade of this Tree of the Great Peace we spread the soft white feathery down of the globe thistle [the great White Mat of the Law, in Dr. Fenton's version] as seats for thee, Atotarho, and thy cousin Lords.

"We place thee upon those seats, spread soft with the feathery down of the globe thistle, there beneath the shade of the spreading branches of the Tree of Peace. There thou shalt sit and watch the Council Fire of the Confederacy of the Five Nations, and all the affairs of the Five Nations shall be transacted at this place before thee, Atotarho, and thy cousin Lords, by the Confederate Lords of the Five Nations."

The constitution of the Great Peace is not a defensive instrument dealing solely with safeguards against oppression and war. It is a positive thing, giving expression to the Five Nations' way of life.

"Our strength shall be in union," said Deganawidah, "and our way the way of reason, righteousness, and peace."

To begin with, it expresses the great principle of unity in diversity, a principle that gave its peculiar strength to the confederacy. Each separate nation, with its individual customs and local pride, knew that its chief assurance of essential independence lay in a union that guaranteed its way of life against all attack.

"The five Council Fires," said Deganawidah, "shall continue to burn as before and they are not quenched."

To the outside world the spirit of the League might seem to be expressed in the Latin motto, *E Pluribus Unum*. But to the nations within the League its spirit might have seemed better expressed in the words, *Ex Uno Plura*. The strength of the whole made safe the individual differences of the members.

If the Kanonsionni, the Longhouse, with its rafters of the Law, protected the five fires, it protected also the rights of the individuals who sat by them. The Iroquois cherished the Four Freedoms of our own day. Two of them received specific mention in the constitution: Freedom from Fear and Freedom from Want.

The avowed purpose of the union was to provide the strength that casts out fear.

"We bind ourselves together," said Deganawidah, "by taking hold of each other's hands so firmly and forming a circle so strong that if a tree should fall upon it, it could not shake nor break it, so that our people and grandchildren shall remain in the circle in security, peace, and happiness."

Freedom from Want was taken care of in the provision that the hunting grounds should be open to all. There was to be common access to raw materials.

"We shall have one dish," said Deganawidah, "in which shall

be placed one beaver's tail, and we shall all have a co-equal right
to it, and there shall be no knife in it, for if there be a knife in it
there will be danger that it might cut someone and blood would
thereby be shed."

Freedom of Religion was regarded among the Five Nations as so
natural a right as to require no mention in the constitution except
in the case of adopted nations, to whom it was specifically granted.
The religion of the Iroquois themselves, which was not unlike
Wordsworth's modified pantheism, was practised without hypoc-
risy or bigotry. Foreign peoples who joined them under the shelter
of the Tree of Peace were allowed, and indeed encouraged, to
worship in their own way. When in the eighteenth century the
Iroquois adopted the tiny remnant of the Tutelo nation, they saw
to it that the beautiful religious observances of this Siouan people
should be preserved. Dr. Frank G. Speck, in his remarkable study,
The Tutelo Spirit Adoption Ceremony, shows how today the Cayugas, under whose wing the Tuteloes were taken some two hundred
years ago, have assumed responsibility for this rite now that there
are no longer any Tutelo-speaking people to attend to it for themselves.

Freedom of Speech was a right so deeply embedded in the
Iroquois way of life as to need no attention in the constitution.
Fires burning all over the Five Nations territory symbolized the
right of public discussion. Besides the Great Council at Onondaga
(the Fire That Never Dies), there were local fires in each nation,
each clan, each family; and the women had their fires as well as the
men.

There was one freedom that the Five Nations denied themselves:
"Freedom, free to slay herself," the liberty to destroy their own
liberties. They knew that great freedom demands, for its preservation, great self-restraint. Being aware how unscrupulous agitators
used the right of free speech to spread diversive propaganda, they
surrounded public debate with safeguards against that danger.

For one thing, the constitution provided that discussion in the
Great Council should not be prolonged after nightfall. The physical
conditions that foster frayed tempers and hasty judgments were
thus avoided.

For another, the public discussion of an important proposition
was not allowed to take place the same day it was received in
council. Time had to be allowed for study of the proposal. When

during that interval, it was seen that serious differences were likely to arise, these were aired in committee. The delegates of each nation discussed the proposal among themselves, compared their conclusions with those of other national groups, and, by tossing the ball back and forth in this manner, they arrived at compromises and accommodations likely to be satisfactory to all concerned. Public debate in the Great Council did not, as a rule, begin until after this preparation; and so, each speaker having been previously instructed by his national delegation (the nation thus speaking "with one voice"), there were seldom heard any of those recriminations from popular leaders which are so apt to set the public by the ears.

There was no designated Bill of Rights, such as is provided in the first amendments to the American Constitution. The rights of man were so thoroughly entrenched in popular custom and everywhere taken so much for granted that any additional guarantees in the constitution seemed unnecessary. The constitution concerned itself less with rights than with duties. This is seen in the means taken to reconcile the principle of equal sovereignty with the facts of nature.

Certain members of the League were more powerful than others, and this fact was frankly recognized in the Longhouse and used to strengthen the structure. The Big Three—Mohawks, Onondagas, and Senecas, the "elder brothers"—were assigned determining rôles in the administration of the League, especially in war and the conduct of foreign affairs. But the constitution found a way, by means of certain checks placed on them and by the balanced use of the veto, to see that none of the Big Three, nor all of them together, should abuse their power.

The Mohawks, a great military nation facing hostile Algonquin tribes to the east, were known as the Keepers of the Eastern Door of the Longhouse, and were accorded a council veto. The Senecas, faced with vast multitudes of alien peoples on the west, were known as the Keepers of the Western Door; and, since they were numerically the strongest of all the Five Nations, it was fitting that they should supply, as they did, the two War Chiefs of the Confederacy. The Onondagas were the Fire Keepers or perpetual hosts. Their chiefs were also the permanent steering committee of the Great Council. They called meetings, prepared the agenda, and provided the chairman or moderator, Atotarho, who rendered decisions in case of disagreement among the other nations and who exercised the power of veto.

The Head Chief of the Onondagas, Atotarho, was Head Chief of the Five Nations; but his authority, and that of succeeding Atotarhoes, was closely circumscribed by the advice of his brother chiefs among the Onondagas and also by the checks embodied in the council procedure as prescribed by the constitution.

Because of certain political exigencies at the time of the founding of the League, some nations had more representatives in the Great Council than others (the Onondagas had fourteen while the Mohawks had nine and the Senecas eight), but this was of no importance since, in the decisions of the Great Council, each nation spoke with only one voice and had only one vote.

Since each of the Five Nations retained its sovereignty, it was necessary for the success of the League that its unity should be of the spirit and reside in the minds of all its citizens. To this end the constitution is filled with poetic symbols.

"We have now completed our power," said Deganawidah at that first Council by Onondaga Lake, "so that we, the Five Nations Confederacy, shall in future have only one body, one head, and one heart."

He gave them the symbol of the Tree, under the shelter of which the Five Nations gathered, and the symbol of the Fire around which they sat. He gave them as a further symbol the Bundle of Arrows, denoting strength through union.

Deganawidah took one arrow from each of the Five Nations, and, tying the arrows together with deer sinews, said: "Now it is completed. I have made it tight. It will be impossible to bend it, and it will endure as long as there shall be generations. . . .

"I say to you it will not be right for one of the several nations to pull out its arrow."

The very name of the League, Kanonsionni, the Longhouse, was a symbol of unity. In the words of the *Jesuit Relations*, the name Kanonsionni signified that the Five Nations "constituted but one family."

Their symbols were not static, but dynamic, looking forward to the growth and extension of the League. The Tree was growing, its Roots were extending, new Braces were being added (by the adoption of foreign peoples) to strengthen the walls of the Longhouse, and new Beams (amendments) were to be added to the

Rafters of the Law. The spirit of progress and adventure united the five families gathered about their separate fires in the Longhouse. They were all crusaders for a better world.

Like Hiawatha they looked forward rather than back: looked forward to an ever-widening community in which the Law should enable reason and justice and peace to prevail, rather than back to the days of national jealousies and war.

As further symbols of an aggressive moral wholeness that should clear the mind of past evils and keep it clear, the council ritual called for a great White Mat or Wampum Belt to be spread on the ground. White wampum signified purity or peace. A great Wing was provided to sweep from the White Wampum Belt any dust or dirt that might adhere to it (the dust and dirt signifying discord). A stick was laid at hand to be used when any creeping thing that might harm their grandchildren was seen approaching the White Wampum Belt. The stick was to remove tricky problems—the seeds of war—before they could reach the council, set the chiefs at odds, and inflame the popular imagination.

"If you chiefs by the council fire," said Deganawidah, "should be continually throwing ashes at one another, your people will go astray, their heads will roll, authority will be gone; your enemies then may see that your minds are scattered, the League will be at a standstill, and the Good News of Peace and Power will be unable to proceed."

Special devices were inserted in the constitution to foster the spirit of union. The Great Council was itself such a device. Meeting not less than once a year, and being called by runners at short notice whenever important business arose, as when a special embassy from a foreign power arrived at Onondaga, the Council was kept constantly in the mind of the common citizen. All persons who cared to were encouraged to attend its meetings—much to the astonishment of the people of Pennsylvania when in 1736 chiefs of the Onondaga Council accompanied by scores of Indian followers sat down by a symbolic fire in the Great Meeting Place in Philadelphia to discuss affairs of state with Thomas Penn.

Meetings of the Great Council were a sight the Indians found well worth seeing. The chiefs in their buckskins (blankets, worn like Roman togas, were used after the white trader arrived on the scene), with coronets of feathers on their heads, sat about the fire in the council house. The meeting was opened with prayer, as prescribed in the constitution, a prayer of thanksgiving to the Creator and to the various manifestation of his Mind in nature.

"Whenever the Confederate Lords shall assemble for the purpose of holding a council," Deganawidah had said, "the Onondaga Lords shall make an address and return thanks to the earth where men dwell, to the streams of water, the pools, the springs, and the lakes, to the maize and the fruits, to the medicinal herbs and trees, to the forest trees for their usefulness, to the animals that serve as food and give their pelts for clothing, to the great winds and the lesser winds, to the Thunderers, to the Sun, the mighty warrior, to the Moon, to the messengers of the Creator who reveal his wishes, and to the Great Creator who dwells in the heavens above, who gives all things useful to man, and who is the source and the ruler of health and life.

"Then shall the Onondaga Lords declare the Council open."

Songs were sung, commemorating the founding of the League; and the music of the beautifully intoned *Jo-hah (U-huy,* as Conrad Weiser described the sound), which circled the fire, the delegates of each nation repeating it in unison as a sign of approval, punctuated all the proceedings.

A colorful and dramatic touch was added by the use of wampum, the white and the purple (or "black"), the latter made from the purple spots in the clam shell. When a chief rose to address the Council, he held in his hand strings of wampum to show that his words were true. They served also as notes for both speaker and audience, helping the one to proceed with and the other to follow the steps in the argument. As each topic was disposed of, the speaker laid down a string of wampum, the strings being afterwards hung on a horizontal pole (such as Hiawatha had used) in the center of the council house for all to see. The speaker who replied took these same strings from the pole and held them in his hand to refresh his memory as he reviewed, point by point, the preceding discourse.

Wampum was venerated among the Iroquois, tradition ascribing its first use to Hiawatha and Deganawidah. "Wampum is our heart," is an Indian saying recorded by Dr. Speck. Wampum gave words authority. Without wampum a message had no validity. To accept wampum was to accept the Word, the message it conveyed.

"They invariably observe this law," reported Father Jogues, a Jesuit missionary among the Mohawks who has since been canonized, "that whoever touches or accepts the present which is made to him is bound to fulfill what is asked of him through that present."

For important matters, such as treaties of peace, belts of wampum were prepared, often of considerable width, with designs inwrought by arrangement of the white and purple beads. Such treaty belts were preserved carefully, the explanation of each being memorized and handed down with the belt itself to succeeding Wampum Keepers, who were the national archivists.

All debate in council was carried on quite literally "across the fire." The Mohawks and Senecas sat on the east side of the fire (the Mohawks north of the Senecas), while the Oneidas and Cayugas sat on the west side (the Oneidas to the north). The Onondagas, as moderators, sat between the two groups, on the north side of the fire.

Propositions were discussed and conclusions arrived at through three separate stages of debate. First, each national delegation discussed the proposition and came to a conclusion so that it might speak with one voice. Second, the national unit compared its conclusions with that of its "brother" (the Mohawk with the Seneca, the Oneida with the Cayuga), in order that each side of the fire might speak with one voice. Then the Mohawks, as representing the Elder Nations, handed the joint decision of Mohawks and Senecas across the fire to the Oneidas, who received it on behalf of the Younger Nations. If the Younger Nations agreed, the matter was handed back across the fire to the Mohawks, who announced the agreement to the Onondagas, and the presiding officer, who inherited the title of "Atotarho," declared the matter settled. If, however, at any stage in this procedure a stubborn disagreement was encountered, the matter was returned for further study to the brotherhoods or to the national units, depending on the point in the line at which the break had occurred. If in the end no agreement could be found, the Mohawks announced this fact to the Onondagas, and they, through the voice of Atotarho, rendered a decision.

The names of the original chiefs, those said to have gathered at that first council by Onondaga Lake, were passed down as titles and so served to strengthen the spirit of unity. The chiefs invested with these titles were living reminders of the story of the founding of the League. There was always a Hiawatha, an Atotarho, a Sharenkhówane, among them—though there was never again to be a Deganawidah, for "There shall be but one Deganawidah," said the father of his country, Deganawidah himself.

The song called "Hail!" (the Iroquois *Hai! Hai!*), which is also known as the "Six Songs" or the "Peace Hymn," served as a further bond of union. It was sung at the national ceremony of condolence and installation, held when a chief died and his successor was invested with the horns of office; but its tone was less one of lamentation than one of thanksgiving: thanksgiving to the League itself, the Great Peace, to their forefathers who had established it, to the men and women who preserved it, and (in the Onondaga version) to the children who should carry it on. Here is the Mohawk version:

THE PEACE HYMN
or
Hai! Hai!
(The Six Songs)

Hai! Hai! Hai!
Hail! Hail! Hail!
    Once more we come to greet and thank the League;
    Once more to greet and thank the nations' Peace.
      Hai, hai, hai, hai, hai!
      Hail, hail, hail, hail, hail!

Hail! Hail! Hail!
    Once more we come to greet and thank the Kindred;
    Once more to greet and thank the dead chief's Kindred.
      Hail, hail, hail, hail, hail!

Hail! Hail! Hail!
    Once more we come to greet and thank the Warriors;
    Once more to greet and thank the nations' Manhood.
      Hail, hail, hail, hail, hail!

Hail! Hail! Hail!
    Once more we come to greet and thank the Women;
    Once more to greet and thank the mourning Women.
      Hail, hail, hail, hail, hail!

Hail! Hail! Hail! that which our Forefathers accomplished!
Hail! Hail! Hail! the Law our Forefathers established!

O listen to us, listen, continue to hear us, our Grandsires!
O listen to us, listen, continue to hear us, our Grandsires!

In *The Iroquois Book of Rites*, Horatio Hale, who calls these verses the National Hymn of the Iroquois, and who suggests that "a comparison between it and other national hymns, whose chief characteristics are self-glorification and defiance, might afford room for some instructive inferences," prints a free translation in the metre of Longfellow's *Hiawatha:*

> To the great Peace bring we greeting!
> To the dead chief's kindred, greeting!
> To the warriors round him, greeting!
> To the mourning women, greeting!
> These our grandsires' words repeating,
> Graciously, O grandsires, hear us!

One of the constitution's best devices for knitting the nations together was the clan system. The relationship between members of a given clan was as binding as that between the members of a family. Yet these clans were inter-tribal. The three clans (in two phratries) that comprised the Mohawk nation (1. Turtle; 2. Bear and Wolf) were the three clans (1. Wolf; 2. Turtle and Bear) that made up the Oneida nation, and they were found as well in all the other nations of the Confederacy. The Onondagas, Cayugas, and Senecas had each a greater number of clans than the Mohawks (the Onondagas nine, the Senecas nine, and the Cayugas ten, including the three Bears: Big Bear, Younger Bear and Suckling Bear), but these nations shared the Deer, Hawk, Heron, Eel, Sandpiper, and other clans among themselves.

Thus a man might travel from the Hudson to the Genesee and never lose touch with his kinsfolk. A Mohawk of the Turtle clan, making a journey to Canandaigua Lake in the Seneca country, would be entertained on the way by his Turtle kin among the Oneidas, Onondagas, Cayugas, and Senecas.

So strictly was this clan-family relationship observed that a man might not marry within his own clan. Our travelling Mohawk, while visiting his Turtle kin abroad, would have to be careful not to fall in love with a Turtle maiden, for he could not marry her. He could marry with Wolf or Bear, but never with Turtle. What's in a name? Nothing, so far as blood or biological law is concerned, but much, to the Iroquois mind, in the realm of the spirit. Intertribal clans meant international goodwill: the drawing together of distant peoples, not by vague phrases about human brotherhood, but by actual ties that touched the personal life.

Responsibility for cultivating the spirit of unity among the people was laid by Deganawidah squarely on the shoulders of the chiefs. By exhortation and example they were to show the way.

"It shall be the duty of all the Five Nations Confederate Lords," said Deganawidah, "from time to time as occasion demands, to act as mentors and spiritual guides of their people and remind them of their Creator's will and words. They shall say:

" 'Hearken, that peace may continue unto future days!

" 'Always listen to the words of the Great Creator, for he has spoken. United people, let no evil find lodging in your minds.

" 'For the Great Creator has spoken and the cause of Peace shall not become old.

" 'The cause of peace shall not die if you remember the Great Creator.' "

If, however, the time ever came, said Deganawidah, that the Fire Dragon of Discord brought division into the Longhouse, and a high wind (war) uprooted the Tree of Peace, then the chiefs were to look for a Great Swamp Elm and, finding one "with large roots extending outwards, bracing outwards from the trunk," they with their people were to take shelter beneath it.

He instructed the chiefs to regard courage, patience, and honesty as the virtues most requisite to their responsibilities; and he urged them to think not so much of present advantage as of the future welfare of their people.

"When you administer the Law," he said, "your skins must be seven thumbs thick. Then the magic darts of your enemies will not penetrate, even if they prod you with their points.

"This is to be of strong mind, O chiefs: Carry no anger and hold no grudges. Think not forever of yourselves, O chiefs, nor of your own generation. Think of continuing generations of our families, think of our grandchildren and of those yet unborn, whose faces are coming from beneath the ground."

World Citizens

IN EXPLAINING the Good News to a chief named Degaihógen, Deganawidah presented a vision of a world community.

"What shall we be like," Degaihogen had asked, "when this Reason and Righteousness and Justice and Health have come?"

"In truth," replied Deganawidah, "Reason brings Righteousness, and Reason is a power that works among all minds alike. When once Reason is established, all the minds of all mankind will be in a state of Health and Peace. It will be as if there were but a single person."

When the Longhouse with Five Fires had been erected and the Tree of Peace planted at Onondaga, Deganawidah's mind leaped forward to the next great adventure: the union, under the shelter of the Tree, of all the nations of mankind. Hiawatha, instructed by Deganawidah, had announced wherever he went on his early mission, that the purpose of the Good News was to make peace and contentment "prevail among the peoples of the whole earth." Now, at the first Council, Deganawidah informed the chiefs that the Tree of Peace had sent forth roots in all directions, the Great White Roots of Peace.

"These roots," he said, "will continue to grow, advancing the Good Mind and Righteousness and Peace, moving into territories of peoples scattered far through the forest. And when a nation, guided by the Great White Roots, shall approach the Tree, you shall welcome her here and take her by the arm and seat her in the place of council. She will add a brace or leaning pole to the Longhouse and will thus strengthen the edifice of Reason and Peace."

Throughout their history the Five Nations have sought to add such braces to the Longhouse: the Tuscaroras of Iroquoian stock from North Carolina, the Nanticokes of Algonquin stock from Maryland's Eastern Shore, and the Tuteloes of Siouan stock from Virginia, by the methods of peace; Hurons, Neutrals, Eries (all of their own stock), and many others, by the methods of war. Foreign nations which, of their own accord, sought shelter under the Tree, were given a generous welcome.

The adoption of the Tuscaroras, "on the cradle-board," was not an unmixed blessing to the Five Nations, who found these new-comers not only populous but also a somewhat obstreperous people.

"A long time ago," said a Seneca councillor to Dr. Fenton, "the Tuscaroras came to us and asked to stop over night. We took the Tuscaroras under our wing, and now they live to itch us like fleas."

Yet, having once accepted them, the Five Nations did not thrust them out. Indeed, they renamed the League the Six Nations when they were adopted, and today the Tuscaroras are an influential part of the Six Nations in western New York as well as in Canada. The "cradle-board" reservation was only a technicality. The Tus-caroras sat in Council and spoke their mind, though through the lips (symbolically) of the nation that sponsored them. In like manner the Nanticokes ("who first founded witchcraft"), the Tuteloes, and the Delawares, when they sat down under the Tree, were allowed to use the voice of the Cayugas, their sponsors, to express their thoughts in the Great Council, their representatives being given seats on the Cayuga side of the fire.

The constitution of the Confederacy provided rules for the adoption of foreign peoples and also for their expulsion if they should attempt in any way to weaken the League. There were rules for inviting nations to enter the Peace, and further rules for making war on them should they decline the invitation.

Even the War Song to be used in extending the Great Peace by force of arms finds a place in that section of the constitution called the Laws of War and Peace:

> . . . I am of the Five Nations
> And I shall make supplication
> To the Almighty Creator.
> He has furnished this army.
> My warriors shall be mighty
> In the strength of the Creator . . .
> For it was he who gave the song,
> This war song that I sing!

Dr. Parker recalls that, when the Eries asked by what power the Five Nations demanded their surrender, the Iroquois replied, "The Master of Life fights for us."

*   *   *   *   *

When the first Council of the United Nations ended, Deganawidah gave the chiefs a farewell in words of both warning and hope.

"If men should ever become indifferent to the League," he said, "perhaps I may stand here again among your descendants. If the Great Peace should fail, call on my name in the bushes, and I will return.

"Now my work is finished. I shall cover my body with bark and bury myself in the ground. There I shall hear how men tend the Longhouse I constructed for them here on the earth.

"These are the number of my words."

With that the man Deganawidah vanishes from sight. Neither history nor legend tells us how, when, or where he died. But we know that, even after he had covered his body with bark and returned to his mother, the Earth, no blood flowed from the sentinel tree at the settlement where he was born. His mission was successful. His work stands.

The Eagle Keeps Watch

SOON enough after the founding of the League, the Eagle that Deganawidah had set on the Tree of Peace to spy out the approach of evil, gave the alarm. The nations surrounding the Iroquois were not friendly. Their many Algonquin neighbors were actively hostile. Adjoining peoples of their own Iroquoian stock, who hemmed them in closely, were hardly less so. The Hurons especially, being far more numerous and in some ways better developed, treated the Five Nations with contempt and great cruelty. To the northeast, east, and south were hordes of Algonquin peoples, Montagnais, Abnakis, Mahicans, Delawares, and others, constantly at war with the upstart Confederacy.

Everywhere the Five Nations were on the defensive. It was to be many years before, first, necessity, and then, success, developed among them the military tradition for which they have later been distinguished.

In the wars with the Adirondacks or Abnakis, whose raids from their strongholds in what is now northern New England had caused, in the opinion of Dr. Parker, the original coming together of the Five Nations, they were entirely successful. On the other hand, the long war with the Ojibways, who dwelt on the north and south shores of Lake Superior, was inconclusive. It ended in a treaty by which the two peoples agreed to live as brothers, but apart. In symbol of this treaty, whenever men of the Five Nations and Ojibways met, they exchanged a special sign of greeting, linking arms in the crook of the elbow. It is said on the Six Nations Reserve that this unusual greeting was reserved exclusively for the Ojibways, and was a mark of peculiar respect.

The Delawares to the south were subjected and given (symbolically) petticoats to wear. As "women" they were denied indulgence in the business of war.

The Mahicans, likewise, who in the late seventeenth century had managed to push the Mohawks far back from the Hudson, were finally defeated and reduced to the status of "nephew," which means "one under control like a package under the arm." Henceforth, like the Delawares, the Mahicans called the Iroquois "uncle."

To the north, meanwhile, there had arisen another and still more dangerous enemy. The French in Canada early in the seventeenth century had seen the spreading influence of the Iroquois, and they were resolved to chop the white roots of the Tree of Peace.

The Five Nations, on the other hand, for long preserved hopes that they might bring the French under the Tree.

"If you love, as you say you do, our souls, love our bodies also," they said, as recorded in the *Jesuit Relations*, "and let us be henceforth but one nation."

But the French, though they honestly desired to see the spread of Christ's gospel of peace throughout America, believed this could best be accomplished by the armies of their Most Christian King. From the days, therefore, of Champlain, the founder of Quebec, they made lavish use of musket and cannon in the endeavor to brush the Five Nations, whom they found to be the chief obstacle to their advance on this continent, out of their way. The Jesuit missionaries, who have left a saga, in the *Jesuit Relations*, of devotion and heroism scarcely to be surpassed, were fiercely prejudiced against the Five Nations, having made their first contacts with Indians among the cruel and jealous enemies of the League. Some, indeed, of the missionaries deprecated the support their order gave the military in return for the clearance of Indian obstacles from the path of their missions. Others, however, approved of it, believing the Cross in America could best be carried forward on the musket barrel, and they expressed a desire for the extermination of the Five Nations. They saw, in the military prowess of the Iroquois, only blood lust and possession of the devil; in their peace talk, only lies and subterfuge; and in their restraint (as well attested by the records as are the cruelties which have made more popular reading), only stupidity.

For many years the Five Nations, under attack by the French, struck back, but not with their full power.

"It is a kind of miracle," wrote a French missionary, "that the Iroquois, although able to destroy us so easily, have not yet done so."

Unfortunately this same missionary, who seems to have known (or understood) nothing about Deganawidah, thought the forbearance of the Iroquois sprang, not from policy, but from inadvertence; and he proposed that the French take advantage of this God-sent blindness, as he believed it to be, to destroy them.

Another missionary, marveling at the lofty ambition of the Five Nations, noted that "they think and say that their own destruction cannot occur without bringing in its train the downfall of the whole earth."

It was not, as the good Father supposed, the possession of fire-arms supplied by the Dutch that had put this lofty idea into Iroquois heads; it was the possession of the dream of world union under their Tree—under the shade, that is, of universal Law. They sincerely believed that unless the nations of the world sat down quietly under the Tree of Peace they would inevitably destroy themselves.

"They proclaim," wrote one of the Jesuit Fathers of a peace embassy the Iroquois proposed to send to Quebec in the spring of 1664, "that they wish to unite all the nations of the earth and to hurl the hatchet so far into the depths of the earth that it shall never be seen in the future; that they wish to place an entirely new Sun in the Heavens, which shall never again be obscured by a single cloud; that they wish to level all the mountains, and remove all the falls from the rivers—in a word, that they wish peace. Moreover, as an evidence of the sincerity of their intentions, they declare that they are coming—women, and children, and old men—to deliver themselves into the hands of the French,—not so much in the way of hostages for their good faith as to begin to make only one Earth and one Nation of themselves and us."

Unfortunately the French and their Indian allies were not yet ready for Deganawidah's vision. When the Iroquois ambassadors, old and reverend men, with their company of women and children bearing gifts of one hundred belts of wampum, some a foot wide, had set out on the long journey to Quebec, the Algonquins laid an ambush for them, killed some, captured others, and put the rest to flight.

"Thus the grand project of this embassy has vanished in smoke," concludes the narrative in the *Jesuit Relations*, "and instead of the peace which it was bringing us, we have on our hands a more cruel war than before."

The hostility of the French was based, in part, on economic grounds. The Hurons were a great trading nation, holding virtual control of the fur trade in the north and west. The French desired, by controlling the Hurons, to keep that trade for themselves. If the Five Nations succeeded in bringing the Hurons under the Great

Tree—making of them "both but one people and only one land," as Father Jogues reported—the Iroquois would insist on sharing their trade. It will be recalled that freedom of trade, the sharing of hunting grounds, was one of the terms of the union.

So the French, using every weapon in the armory of power politics and secret diplomacy (their soldiers, governors, merchants, missionaries, ambassadors, and Indian allies were all agents of "the most Christian King"), persisted in thwarting the efforts of the Five Nations to extend their alliances to the north. The Hurons, at times, showed a desire for the alliance, but it always happened that their negotiations were blocked, or, if these were concluded, that the agreement itself was afterwards nullified. The Great White Roots extending to the north were constantly hacked at by secret enemies.

"Whenever a person or persons of other nations," Deganawidah had said, "shall cut or hack any of these four great roots [north, east, south, and west] which grow from the Great Tree we have planted . . . then shall great trouble come into the seat of you Lords of the Confederacy."

By 1642 the Five Nations knew they were in great danger. The Hurons, secure in their numbers and the wealth the fur trade brought them, and comfortably assured of the support of the French and their circle of Indian allies, especially of the Andastes or Susquehannocks whose armies and fortified towns (supplied with cannon) posed a deadly threat to the southern flank of the Iroquois, had become indifferent to peace with the Five Nations. The French, with the assistance of the Jesuit missionaries, were tying a noose about the Confederacy.

The constitution contained a provision for just such an emergency.

"Should a great calamity threaten the generations rising and living of the Five United Nations, then he who is able to climb to the top of the Tree of the Great Long Leaves [the Tree of Peace] may do so. When, then, he reaches the top of the Tree he shall look about in all directions, and, should he see that evil things are indeed approaching, then shall he call to the people of the Five United Nations assembled beneath the Tree of the Great Long Leaves and say, 'A calamity threatens your happiness.'

"Then shall the Lords convene in council and discuss the impending evil."

The chiefs in council did discuss this evil, and it was decided to send north an embassy proposing peace to all the nations of those parts, French, Huron, Algonquin, and Montagnais.

Again the constitution gave directions:

"When the proposition to establish the Great Peace is made to a foreign nation, it shall be done in mutual council. The foreign nation is to be persuaded by reason and urged to come into the Great Peace."

Such a council was, accordingly, proposed and arranged for at Three Rivers on the St. Lawrence in Canada. Preparations were made by the Five Nations with great care, for they were resolved that the conference should be decisive, either for peace or war. It was so ordained in the constitution:

"When the Confederate Council of the Five Nations has for its object the establishment of the Great Peace among the people of an outside nation and that nation refuses to accept the Great Peace, then by such refusal they bring a declaration of war upon themselves from the Five Nations. Then shall the Five Nations seek to establish the Great Peace by a conquest of the rebellious nation."

The destinies of North America hung on the outcome of the conference at Three Rivers.

The Iroquois ambassadors were well supported. Some five hundred warriors accompanied the delegation and erected fortifications on the south shore of the St. Lawrence—again with faithful adherence to the words of the constitution:

"When the Lords of the Five Nations propose to meet in conference with a foreign nation with proposals for an acceptance of the Great Peace, a large body of warriors shall conceal themselves in a secure place safe from the espionage of the foreign nation but as near at hand as possible."

Three canoes were sent across the river to meet the French, once more in such close compliance with instructions in the constitution as to show how firmly the Great Law was implanted in the minds of those who wore the antlers at Onondaga.

"Two warriors shall accompany the Union Lord who carries the proposals, and these warriors shall be especially cunning. Should the Lord be attacked, these warriors shall hasten back to the army of warriors with the news of the calamity which befell by the treachery of the foreign nation."

The remainder of the story may best be told in the words of the *Jesuit Relations.* The missionary Le Jeune described the incident faithfully, without, however, in the least understanding it, since he and the rest of the French, misled by an Indian informer (one of the Montagnais, who lived north and west of Three Rivers in the Saguenay region), allowed themselves to see nothing but treachery in the words and acts of Deganawidah's followers.

The three canoes "moved up and down before the fort, within hearing," writes Le Jeune; "one of the oldest men belonging to this squadron cried with a loud voice, speaking to the Savages: 'Listen to me! I come to treat for peace with all the Nations of these parts, with the Montagnais, with the Algonquins, with the Hurons; the land shall be beautiful, the river shall have no more waves, one may go everywhere without fear.'"

No generous nor even adequate response to this appeal was forthcoming, though it had been made in the spirit, and almost in the words, of Deganawidah. Instead, an Algonquin Indian came out on the bank and called the Iroquois sachem a liar.

The Governor of New France, Monsieur the Chevalier de Montmagny (i.e., Big Mountain, which in the Iroquois tongue is *Onóntio* —a name the Indians gave to all succeeding governors of New France), now appeared on the scene and, being averse to risking his person among those whom he deemed savages, despatched delegates to a conference which was to be held on the Iroquois side of the river.

The French delegates found themselves received in full council, the Indians sitting in a circle about a symbolic fire as the constitution prescribed. For the second time peace was proposed by the Five Nations.

Onágan, a chief, speaking with great earnestness and dignity, though not without a touch of the humor that so often warms Iroquois rhetoric, sent the Governor renewed proposals for a peace that should be all-embracing.

Taking "the hands of Father Ragueneau and of the sieur Nicolet, the delegates to negotiate peace," writes Le Jeune, "then touching them on the face and on the chin, he said to them, 'Not only shall our customs be your customs, but we shall be so closely united that our chins shall be reclothed with hair, and with beards like yours.'"

The Governor, having delayed his reply considerably beyond the time agreed on, at length approached the south bank with several shallops filled with armed men; but he declined to go ashore. The Iroquois, accordingly, sent out a canoe containing three chiefs, who, presenting belts of wampum to show that their words were true, proposed for a third time a peace which should include the French and their Indian allies.

The Governor, haughty and insulting, hedged in his reply and, believing that the Iroquois offers were motivated solely by a fear of French arms, ventured a show of force.

Whereupon the Iroquois raised above their fortification on the bank an Algonquin scalp as a declaration of war, and proceeded to make their own show of force in a manner to cause Montmagny mountains of astonishment. Portaging their canoes to avoid a trap the Governor had laid for them with his armed vessels, and retiring to the shelter of stronger and better-manned fortifications in the woods than the French had dreamed of, they proceeded to work for peace by methods they were assured the white man would understand better than he understood the etiquette of Deganawidah's peace council.

"Thus," concludes Le Jeune, "the war with these tribes has broken out more fiercely than ever."

The Iroquois gave a good account of themselves.

"It is therefore a marvel," we read elsewhere in the *Jesuit Relations*, "that so few people work such great havoc and render themselves so redoubtable to so large a number of tribes . . ."

Throughout the proceedings at Three Rivers in 1642, even in their military dispositions, the Five Nations had followed both the spirit and the letter of Deganawidah's constitution, their guide to international law. That same law had taught them that war and conquest were never to be regarded as ends in themselves. The Five Nations, accordingly, did not give up hope of ultimate peace with the French. Three years after the Three Rivers fiasco, the war in the meantime not having been pushed to the extreme of which they were capable, the Five Nations tried again for peace.

At Three Rivers in 1645, the Mohawk chief, Kiotsaeton, made another appeal in the spirit of Deganawidah. In a moving address he referred to passing, as he came north for the conference, "the place where the Algonquins massacred us last Spring . . . I turned away my eyes for fear of exciting my anger," he continued; "then, striking the earth and listening, I heard the voice of my Forefathers massacred by the Algonquins. When they saw that my heart was capable of seeking revenge they called out to me in a loving voice: 'My grandson, my grandson, be good; do not get angry. Think no longer of us for there is no means of withdrawing us from death. Think of the living—that is of importance; save those who still live from the sword and fire that pursue them; one living man is better than many dead ones.' After having heard those voices I passed on, and I came to you, to deliver those whom you still hold."

Kiotsaeton asked for the return of prisoners, presented wampum to clear the river of waves, and invited the French and their allies to join them in a peace that should be cemented by trade. His mission was successful.

But the peace concluded was not a lasting one. The Hurons, who were included in it, continued to keep their trade to themselves. Next year, 1646, the whole Huron fur fleet went to Montreal, and the furs they could not sell there (for lack of goods among the French inhabitants sufficient to buy such quantities of pelts) went back to the Huron country. Observing that, the Iroquois understood that to the Hurons peace meant no more than an armistice, a cessation of fighting, and not the brotherliness and good sense of Deganawidah's vision. To the Five Nations peace and trade were inseparable.

When in 1647 the Five Nations learned further that the Hurons had made an aggressive alliance with the Susquehannocks, who promised to "lift the axe" whenever the Hurons called on them to do so, they knew there was only one way. *Delenda est Carthago:* the Hurons must be destroyed.

Of what happened to that unhappy people, once the Five Nations had made up their minds, the *Jesuit Relations* bear mournful witness. In 1649 the Hurons ceased to exist as a nation.

The real enemy was still France, and the Five Nations proceeded to weaken her further by depriving her of the more powerful of her remaining Indian allies. They marked the whole Huron circle for extinction. In a series of campaigns which is one of the near miracles of North American military history, they put out of business the Tobacco Nation, the Neutrals, the Eries, and finally, in 1675, the mighty Susquehannocks.

These people were all defeated and dispersed, some fleeing to far nations for refuge and others coming in, as the Five Nations had always hoped they would do, to receive welcome and shelter under the Tree of Peace. These latter were adopted, and formed thereafter strong props to the Longhouse.

Whole villages of Hurons reëstablished themselves comfortably in the Seneca country, where the Jesuit missionaries soon after found them and renewed acquaintanceship with old friends from the Georgian Bay region. A remnant of the Susquehannocks, adopted by the Oneidas, became so thoroughly at home among them that they gave up their own language and spoke Oneida. Yet they never altogether lost their national identity. Many years later they were sent back to their old territory in the Susquehanna Valley, establishing themselves at Conestoga, near Lancaster, Pennsylvania, where they remained till the Paxton Boys, a band of frontier ruffians from the neighborhood of today's Harrisburg, wiped them out in the massacres of 1763.

Those were the great days of Iroquois military history. The Five Nations had shown that a disposition to peace need not breed softness, and that Peace armed with Power and guided by Reason is irresistible. In less than thirty years they had broken the ring forged around them. Guided by the Eagle That Sees Afar, they had invaded Canada, defied the power of France, and destroyed her Indian allies. They were now the guardians of the peace throughout the woods of eastern North America. Their Tree stood firm, and, as they said, "spread its roots to a vast distance."

When the French, following Denonville's expedition of 1687 from across Lake Ontario against the Senecas, claimed title to the Iroquois country, the Five Nations made a neat reply. They admitted that the French had formerly come to the Mohawk country, as they had more recently come to the Seneca country, where they had burnt some bark houses and cut down the corn; but, they added, "if that be a good title, then we can claim all Canada."

Twilight

THE French in Canada, growing in numbers, continued to hack at the roots of the Great Tree.

The Sieur de la Barre, Governor of Canada, writing from Quebec, October 1, 1684, indicated his intention to bring division into the Longhouse, "and for this purpose to send persons expressly to communicate my sentiments to the Revd Jesuit Fathers who are missionaries and to request them to act."

French troops under Denonville invaded the Longhouse, burned the stockades, destroyed some 1,200,000 bushels of Indian corn, and carried away the wampum records.

The Five Nations were not broken. The people of their towns, forewarned of the French attack, had vanished into the woods, and their armies were still intact. They pursued the French and recovered most of the wampum. Two years later they were strong enough to inflict fearful retribution at Lachine, when fifteen hundred warriors, having concealed their penetration of the settlements, suddenly emerged with a whoop to lay waste the country up to the very palisades of Montreal, burning houses, killing over two hundred people, taking ninety prisoners, and immobilizing French garrisons for as many weeks as the warriors chose to delay their departure.

Nevertheless the Five Nations had been shaken by Denonville's expedition, as they were to be shaken again by Frontenac's destruction in 1696 of Onondaga, their palisaded capital. Their towns (or castles, as the Dutch called them), perched on hill platforms behind wall and moat, were never again built in the old proud way. The white man's cannon had made wooden stockades seem ridiculous.

They knew the twilight was setting in. Their songs bear pathetic witness to that knowledge.

Hail, my grandsires! Now hearken while your grandchildren cry mournfully to you,—because the Great League which you established has grown old. . . .

O my grandsires! Even now that has become old which you established, the Great League. You have it as a pillow under your heads in the ground where you are lying, this Great League which you established;

[53]

although you said that far away in the future the Great League would endure.

It may seem strange to us today that this tiny people (the total population of the Five Nations never exceeded fifteen thousand, men, women, and children) should ever have dreamed of world union under their Tree. Certainly the causes of their failure to establish such a world union are evident enough.

To begin with, they had little control over their young warriors. Against the judgment of the sachems or chiefs who wore the antlers and tended the Fire at Onondaga, raiding parties composed of young hotheads broke the peace among their Indian neighbors, even among some, such as the Catawbas, while they were actually tracing the roots of the Tree of Peace to their source, i.e., seeking peace with the Iroquois. Such unauthorized war parties inevitably revived old resentments and impeded the restoration of Reason. A greater discipline over their own people than their views on liberty permitted was necessary if the Tree of Peace was to continue to grow.

Another cause of failure lay in the conservatism of later generations, who declined to widen the basis of representation on the Great Council so as to admit chiefs of adopted nations as a matter of right and not of mere courtesy. No doubt they were afraid lest a diluted Council might lack the moral unity and strength of a Council composed of delegates from nations that of old had been imbued with the spirit of Deganawidah. But that restriction made it difficult for other nations to enter without surrendering their pride. To ask strong peoples to allow themselves to be brought in "on the cradle-board" was not, in the words of Deganawidah, to "dip with the current" but to go against nature.

A few years ago the Canadian government attempted to remedy this defect in the Iroquois representative system by providing for strictly democratic election to the Council; but the pride of the Six Nations was offended by the brusque manner in which the new constitution was thrust upon them, and a section of them has given the reform a none-too-sympathetic reception. There is today on the Grand River (Six Nations) Reserve a movement to restore Deganawidah's roster of chiefs.

The principal shortcoming of the old Five Nations, as leaders of a world community, was of course lack of knowledge, their failure to reckon with the vast number and complexity of the nations of the world. They had had no Columbus to discover Europe for them. However advanced their political conceptions might be, their civilization was of the Stone Age, and could scarcely be expected to cope successfully with, much less to assimilate, peoples of the Iron Age when they burst upon them.

Even before the seventeenth century, with all its triumphs, had passed, the Five Nations had come to know that they could not, by themselves, forever control the swarms of white people who came in "great canoes" from across the sea and hacked continually at their roots.

At New York in 1684 the Five Nations made an appeal, on grounds of justice and brotherhood, to the English to help them hold their territory against the French.

"Your Sachem [the King] is a great Sachem," they said, "and we are but a small people. When the English came to Manhatans, that is, New York, [to] Aragiske, which is now Virginia, and to Jaquokranaegare, now called Maryland, they were a small people and we a great people; and, finding they were good people, we gave them land and treated them civilly; and now, since you are a great people and we but small, you will protect us from the French, which if you do not, we shall lose all our hunting and beavers."

During the eighteenth century, in the hope of preserving yet a little longer the friendly way of life they enjoyed among themselves but which they already saw was doomed to be burnt out by the fierce blast of the white man's competition, they played a skillful diplomatic game, holding the balance of power between the French and English in America—dipping the scales somewhat toward the English, who had long been their good ally.

The Tree, meanwhile, was losing its world significance, though it remained the symbol of friendship between individual nations. They planted it wherever they made a treaty.

"We have the Tree of Peace and Tranquillity in this place," they said at Albany, "which Tree hath shaked and quaked much of late; we establish that Tree firm and strong that in the future it may not be in a wavering condition but immovable. . . . Now we make the Root to the said Tree that it may flourish and that the Root may extend itself as far as to the Senecas country."

It was under the Tree at Albany, which they said they hoped "might thrive and spread itself beyond Canada," that they most frequently found shelter; and in the wars between the French and English, ending in 1763 with the retirement of Onontio (France) from Canada, they supported the British cause.

When the Revolution came, they were in the midst of the first long period of prosperity they had ever enjoyed. Towns were flourishing, their houses were modern, their farms and orchards productive. They had no wish to enter the white man's quarrel, and they had much sympathy with the people of the "Thirteen Fires," as they called the American colonies; but the covenants they had made and the chains of friendship they had brightened for many years past with the English-speaking peoples had all been in the name of the Great Sachem, the King. It was their pride as a people to keep covenant. When they found that the English spoke with two voices, they were "become miserable." When actual war broke out, their councils were divided. But they had learned long since, in the words of Scaróyady, the "Half King" or viceregent they had once set over their own colony on the Ohio, that "you cannot live in the woods and stay neutral." Old loyalties prevailed, and they threw their weight on the side of the King.

In defeat they left behind them the hills and lakes they loved, and travelled away from the sunrise. Beyond Niagara they received from the King new lands beside the Grand River, once their favorite waterway to the far west; and there they found the Great Swamp Elm, which Deganawidah had said should give them shelter if ever a high wind uprooted the Great White Pine—the Tree of Peace.

They rebuilt the Longhouse, and preserved as well as they could in the narrow confines of the Six Nations Reserve at Brantford, Ontario, and after the loss of most of their wampum, the glorious traditions of Deganawidah and Hiawatha. A great part of their people remained in the country of the Thirteen Fires. Joseph Brant, their war chief who had led them to Canada, even sent his son back to New England, to Dr. Wheelock's school (now Dartmouth College) for his education. The Canadian branch never wholly severed its family connections across the border. The clan-family relationship recognizes no international boundary.

Their capital is now at Ohswéken, Ont., where a new Council House preserves the memory of the Fire That Never Dies. The language they use in council is English, and their Atotarho, or presiding officer, is an official of the Canadian government. But they speak their native tongue in their homes, and privately install chiefs according to the ritual of Deganawidah.

They are up-to-date farmers, stock-breeders, and business men. They even drill for natural gas. But the dream of Deganawidah has not died out among them.

"We were once a great people," said a Mohawk a few years ago on the Reserve. "God punished us for our sins. But we shall rise again and the world will listen to us."

1450

ONONDAGA

Roots have spread out
from the Tree of the Great Peace . . .

1945

SAN FRANCISCO

We the peoples of the United Nations
determined to save succeeding generations
from the scourge of war . . .
and to reaffirm faith in fundamental human rights . . .
and to establish conditions under which
justice and respect for law
can be maintained . . .
do hereby establish an international organization
to be known as the United Nations.